contents

Please note that Australian cup and
spoon measurements are metric.
A conversion chart appears on page 62.

potato wedges

5 large oval-shaped potatoes (1.5kg)
cooking-oil spray

1 Preheat oven to 200°C/180°C fan-forced. Line oven tray with baking paper.
2 Halve potatoes lengthways; cut each half into three wedges. Boil, steam or microwave wedges, covered, 5 minutes; drain.
3 Place wedges on tray; spray with oil. Cook, uncovered, in oven, about 30 minutes or until browned, turning occasionally.

preparation time 10 minutes
cooking time 40 minutes
serves 10
notes Wedges can be prepared up to three hours ahead; bake just before serving. We used desiree potatoes for this recipe.

mini beef meatballs

1kg beef mince
1 cup (70g) stale breadcrumbs
½ cup (40g) coarsely grated parmesan cheese
2 cloves garlic, crushed
2 green onions, sliced thinly
1 tablespoon worcestershire sauce
2 tablespoons barbecue sauce
2 tablespoons olive oil

1 Combine beef, breadcrumbs, cheese, garlic, onion and sauces in large bowl; shape level tablespoons of mixture into balls.
2 Heat oil in large frying pan; cook meatballs, in batches, until cooked through. Drain on absorbent paper.
3 Serve meatballs with tomato sauce or sweet chilli sauce, if you like.

preparation time 25 minutes
cooking time 20 minutes
makes about 50
notes Meatballs can be cooked one day ahead; keep, covered, in the refrigerator. Reheat meatballs, in a single layer, on oven trays, covered loosely with foil, in oven (180°C/160°C fan-forced) for about 10 minutes. Uncooked meatballs can be frozen between layers of freezer wrap for up to three months; thaw in refrigerator for 12 hours or overnight before cooking as per recipe.

mini pizzas with 3 toppings

1 cup (280g) tomato paste
12 x 225g mini pizza bases
ham and pineapple
1½ cups (150g) pizza cheese
150g leg ham, chopped
coarsely
1 cup (180g) drained canned
pineapple pieces
vegetarian
1½ cups (150g) pizza cheese
½ cup (120g) coarsely
chopped char-grilled
capsicum
¼ cup (30g) seeded black
olives, sliced thinly
50g button mushrooms,
sliced thinly
⅓ cup (50g) drained
semi-dried tomatoes in oil,
chopped coarsely
chicken, broccoli and
sweet chilli
1 cup (85g) small broccoli
florets
1½ cups (150g) pizza cheese
2 cups (320g) shredded
cooked chicken
¼ cup (60ml) sweet chilli sauce

1 Preheat oven to 200°C/180°C fan-forced.
2 Spread 1 tablespoon of the tomato paste over each pizza base. Place bases on oven trays; sprinkle with toppings, as instructed below. Bake about 20 minutes or until browned lightly.

ham and pineapple Sprinkle 1 cup of the cheese over four pizza bases. Top with ham, pineapple then remaining cheese.

vegetarian Sprinkle 1 cup of the cheese over four pizza bases. Top with capsicum, olives, mushrooms and tomato then remaining cheese.

chicken, broccoli and sweet chilli Drop broccoli into small saucepan of boiling water; return to the boil, drain. Sprinkle 1 cup of the cheese over four pizza bases. Top with chicken and remaining cheese; bake as instructed. Serve sprinkled with broccoli and sauce.

preparation time 20 minutes
cooking time 20 minutes
makes 12
note Each of the toppings makes enough for four pizza bases.

chicken, avocado and cream cheese sandwich

¼ cup (40g) coarsely chopped cooked chicken
¼ small avocado (50g), chopped coarsely
1 teaspoon lemon juice
1 tablespoon spreadable cream cheese
2 slices multigrain bread (90g)
60g mesclun

1 Combine chicken, avocado and juice in small bowl.
2 Spread cream cheese on one bread slice; top with chicken mixture, mesclun and remaining bread slice.

preparation time 10 minutes
makes 1 sandwich

chicken and vegetable pasties

2 teaspoons vegetable oil
2 cloves garlic, crushed
1 medium brown onion (150g), chopped finely
1½ cups (240g) coarsely chopped leftover cooked chicken
2 cups (240g) frozen pea, corn and carrot mixture
2 teaspoons dijon mustard
½ cup (120g) sour cream
¼ cup (30g) coarsely grated cheddar cheese
4 sheets ready-rolled puff pastry
1 egg, beaten lightly

1 Preheat oven to 220°C/200°C fan-forced. Lightly oil oven tray.
2 Heat oil in large frying pan; cook garlic and onion, stirring, until onion softens.
3 Add chicken, frozen vegetables, mustard, sour cream and cheese to pan; stir until hot.
4 Cut one 22cm round from each pastry sheet. Place a quarter of the filling in centre of each round. Brush edge of pastry with egg; fold over to enclose filling, pinching edge together to seal.
5 Place pasties on tray; brush with remaining egg. Bake, in oven, about 30 minutes or until browned lightly.

preparation time 15 minutes
cooking time 30 minutes
serves 4

canapés with three toppings

80g packet mini toasts
ham and cheese
2 tablespoons cheese spread
2 slices (30g) shaved leg ham,
  cut into 1.5cm strips
1 teaspoon finely chopped
  fresh flat-leaf parsley
hummus and carrot
2 tablespoons hummus
2 tablespoons finely grated
  carrot
12 fresh coriander leaves
**cream cheese and
  sweet chilli**
¼ cup (90g) spreadable
  cream cheese, softened
2 teaspoons finely chopped
  fresh flat-leaf parsley
1 tablespoon sweet chilli sauce

ham and cheese Spread most of the cheese over 12 mini toasts; top with rolled ham then a small dollop of the remaining cheese. Sprinkle with parsley.

hummus and carrot Spread hummus over 12 mini toasts; top with carrot then coriander.

cream cheese and sweet chilli Combine cream cheese and parsley in small bowl. Spoon mixture into piping bag fitted with a medium plain tube; pipe cream cheese mixture on remaining toasts. Drizzle each with a little sweet chilli sauce.

preparation time 25 minutes
makes 36
notes Canapés can be made an hour ahead; keep, covered, in the refrigerator. Canapés are not suitable to freeze.
Instead of piping the cream cheese onto the canapés, just dollop on using a teaspoon.

chicken spring rolls

16 x 12.5cm spring roll wrappers
1 egg, beaten lightly
vegetable oil, for deep-frying
filling
2 teaspoons vegetable oil
150g chicken mince
1 clove garlic, crushed
1cm piece fresh ginger (5g), grated
2 green onions, chopped finely
1 small carrot (70g), grated finely
½ cup (40g) coarsely chopped bean sprouts
1 tablespoon oyster sauce

1 Make filling.
2 Place level tablespoons of filling along bottom edge of each wrapper; brush edges with egg, roll to enclose filling, folding in sides of wrapper.
3 Deep-fry rolls, in batches, in hot oil until browned lightly; drain on absorbent paper.
4 Serve rolls with sweet chilli sauce, if you like.
filling Heat oil in medium frying pan; stir-fry chicken, garlic and ginger until chicken is browned lightly. Remove from heat; stir in onion, carrot, sprouts and sauce, cool.

preparation time 15 minutes (+ cooling time)
cooking time 30 minutes
makes 16
notes Spring rolls can be cooked one day ahead; keep, covered, in the refrigerator. Reheat rolls, in a single layer, on oven trays, covered loosely with foil, in oven (180°C/160°C fan-forced) for about 10 minutes.

bean nachos

420g can mexican-style beans, rinsed, drained
290g can kidney beans, rinsed, drained, mashed
2 tablespoons tomato paste
¼ cup (60ml) water
230g packet plain corn chips
1½ cups (180g) coarsely grated cheddar cheese
1 large avocado (320g)
1 tablespoon lemon juice
1 small red onion (100g), chopped finely
1 large tomato (220g), chopped finely
½ cup (120g) sour cream
2 tablespoons fresh coriander leaves

1 Preheat oven to 200°C/180°C fan-forced.
2 Heat combined beans, paste and the water, stirring, in large frying pan.
Remove from heat; cover to keep warm.
3 Place corn chips in individual ovenproof dishes; sprinkle with cheese,
Bake, in oven, about 5 minutes or until cheese melts.
4 Meanwhile, mash avocado in small bowl; stir in juice, onion and tomato.
5 Top heated corn chips with bean mixture, avocado mixture and sour cream;
sprinkle nachos with coriander, and cracked black pepper, if you like.

preparation time 15 minutes
cooking time 10 minutes
serves 10
notes Nachos is best made just before serving. Prepare nachos in
large ovenproof dish, rather than individual dishes, if you prefer.

baby BLTs

12 "bake at home" dinner rolls (40g)
6 rindless bacon rashers (390g)
⅓ cup (100g) mayonnaise
2 small tomatoes (180g), sliced thinly
1 coral lettuce, leaves separated

1 Preheat oven to 180°C/160°C fan-forced.
2 Place bread rolls on oven tray; bake 5 minutes. Split rolls in half almost all the way through.
3 Meanwhile, cut bacon in half crossways; cook bacon in heated large frying pan until crisp. Drain on absorbent paper.
4 Just before serving, spread mayonnaise on rolls; fill rolls with tomato, bacon and lettuce.

preparation time 15 minutes
cooking time 15 minutes
makes 12

fish & chips

2kg large oval potatoes, peeled
cooking-oil spray
12 firm white fish fillets (1.2kg)
¼ cup (35g) plain flour
1 egg
¼ cup (60ml) milk
1 cup (70g) stale breadcrumbs
½ cup (80g) corn flake crumbs

1 Preheat oven to 200°C/180°C fan-forced.
2 Cut potatoes lengthways into 1.5cm-thick slices; cut slices into 1cm-thick chips. Place chips, in single layer, on oiled oven tray; spray with oil. Cook, uncovered, about 40 minutes or until chips are browned and tender.
3 Meanwhile, cut each fish fillet into three pieces. Toss pieces in flour, shake off excess. Dip fish pieces in combined egg and milk then toss in combined crumbs. Place fish on oiled oven tray; spray with oil.
4 Bake fish, uncovered, for the final 15 minutes of chip baking time.

preparation time 35 minutes
cooking time 40 minutes
serves 12
notes Fish can be crumbed, ready for baking, up to three hours ahead of cooking time; keep, covered, in the refrigerator.
Potatoes can be prepared up to three hours ahead of cooking time; keep, covered, in water. Drain and dry potatoes well before cooking.

chicken burritos

1¼ cups (200g) coarsely chopped cooked chicken
¼ cup (75g) mayonnaise
¼ cup (60g) sour cream
1 cup (60g) finely shredded lettuce
2 small tomatoes (180g), chopped finely
½ cup (60g) coarsely grated cheddar cheese
3 x 20cm flour tortillas

1 Combine chicken, mayonnaise and sour cream in medium bowl.
2 Divide chicken mixture, lettuce, tomato and cheese among tortillas; roll tightly to enclose filling. Cut tortillas in half to serve.

preparation time 20 minutes
makes 6 half-burritos
note The filling can be made up to two days in advance; store, in an airtight container, in the refrigerator.

heart-shaped hamwiches

18 large slices white sandwich bread (810g)
⅓ cup (80g) spreadable cream cheese
100g shaved ham

1 Using 7.5cm heart cutter, cut two hearts from each slice of bread.
Using 4cm heart cutter, cut a smaller heart from the centre of half the
large hearts.
2 Spread one side of the large uncut hearts with some of the cream
cheese; top with ham. Spread the remaining cream cheese on one
side of the remaining hearts; place on top of ham.

preparation time 30 minutes
makes 18
notes You need a loaf of the larger-sized bread (slices measure 12cm across).
Sandwiches can be made three hours ahead; keep, covered, in the
refrigerator. Use the heart cutter to cut-out heart shapes from ham for a
really neat fit. Ham slices can be used instead of the shaved ham, if you
like. The little cut-out hearts can be used to make fairy bread.

turkey and cream cheese roll-ups

1 piece lavash bread (60g)
1 tablespoon spreadable cream cheese
3 slices (65g) smoked turkey
3 cheese slices
3 iceberg lettuce leaves
1 small egg tomato (60g), sliced thinly

1 Spread bread with cream cheese. Place turkey, cheese, lettuce and tomato on bread; roll tightly to enclose filling. Cut in half to serve.

preparation time 5 minutes
makes 2 roll-ups

gingerbread biscuits

125g butter, chopped
⅓ cup (75g) firmly packed
  brown sugar
½ cup (175g) golden syrup
3 cups (450g) plain flour
2 teaspoons ground ginger
2 teaspoons ground cinnamon
½ teaspoon ground clove
2 teaspoons bicarbonate
  of soda
1 egg, beaten lightly
1 teaspoon vanilla extract
sparkling cachous, to decorate
royal icing
2 egg whites
3 cups (480g) pure icing sugar
food colourings

notes To make a quick piping
bag, snip a corner off a small
plastic bag.
Un-iced biscuits can be made
three days ahead; store in
an airtight container. Freeze
un-iced biscuits between layers
of freezer wrap for up to one
month. Thaw biscuits at room
temperature for one hour.

1 Preheat oven to 180°C/160°C fan-forced.
Grease and line oven trays with baking paper.
2 Combine butter, sugar and golden syrup
in small saucepan; stir over low heat until
smooth. Cool 5 minutes.
3 Sift flour, spices and soda into large bowl;
add butter mixture, egg and extract, stir until
mixture is combined.
4 Knead dough on floured surface until smooth.
Roll dough between sheets of baking paper to
5mm thickness; refrigerate 10 minutes.
5 Using round, heart and star-shaped cutters,
cut out shapes from dough; place on trays.
6 Bake about 10 minutes or until browned.
Cool on trays.
7 Meanwhile, make royal icing.
8 Decorate biscuits by spreading or piping
with royal icing; decorate with cachous.
royal icing Beat egg whites in small bowl with
electric mixer until frothy; gradually beat in
sifted icing sugar, a tablespoon at a time, until
stiff peaks form. Tint icing as desired. Keep
icing covered with a damp cloth, or enclosed
tightly in plastic piping bags; the icing will
develop a crust once it's exposed to the air.

preparation time 30 minutes
cooking time 10 minutes
makes about 20

strawberry & cream meringues

2 egg whites
½ cup (110g) caster sugar
1 teaspoon white vinegar
2 teaspoons icing sugar
pink food colouring
½ cup (125ml) thickened cream, whipped
3 large strawberries, sliced thinly

1 Preheat oven to 120°C/100°C fan-forced. Grease two oven trays; dust with cornflour, shake off excess.
2 Beat egg whites in small bowl with electric mixer until soft peaks form. Gradually add caster sugar, 1 tablespoon at a time, beating until dissolved between additions. Fold in vinegar, sifted icing sugar and a few drops of pink food colouring.
3 Drop rounded tablespoons of meringue mixture, 3cm apart, on oven trays. Using the back of a teaspoon, make a small hollow in each meringue.
4 Bake meringues about 30 minutes. Cool meringues in oven with door ajar.
5 Just before serving, fill meringues with cream and top with strawberries.

preparation time 25 minutes (+ cooling time)
cooking time 30 minutes
makes 12
notes Meringues can be made one day ahead; store, in an airtight container, at room temperature.

luscious lolly lips

3 cups (105g) rice bubbles
360g white eating chocolate, melted
40 lolly lips

1 Grease 20cm x 30cm lamington pan; line base and two long sides
with baking paper, extending paper 5cm above edges.
2 Combine rice bubbles and chocolate in large bowl. Press mixture
firmly into pan. Press lips, 5 across and 8 down, firmly onto slice.
Refrigerate 1 hour or until set before cutting.

preparation time 10 minutes (+ refrigeration time)
makes 40
note Slice can be made two days ahead; store in an airtight container.
A lamington pan is a 20cm x 30cm slab cake pan, 3cm deep. You can
use a rectangular slice pan of the same dimensions instead.

hedgehog slice

¾ cup (180ml) sweetened condensed milk
60g butter
125g dark eating chocolate, chopped coarsely
125g plain sweet biscuits
⅓ cup (50g) unsalted roasted peanuts
⅓ cup (55g) sultanas

1 Grease 8cm x 26cm bar pan; line base and long sides with baking paper, extending paper 5cm above edges.
2 Combine condensed milk and butter in small saucepan; stir over low heat until smooth. Remove from heat, add chocolate; stir until smooth.
3 Break biscuits into small pieces in a large bowl. Add nuts and sultanas; stir in the chocolate mixture.
4 Spread mixture into pan; refrigerate 3 hours or until firm. Remove from pan before slicing.

preparation time 10 minutes (+ refrigeration time)
cooking time 5 minutes
makes 18
note Slice can be made three days ahead; store, in an airtight container, in the refrigerator.

king of the jungle cupcakes

340g packet buttercake mix
butter cream
125g butter, softened
1½ cups (240g) icing sugar
2 tablespoons milk
caramel food colouring
decorations
5 x 50g Violet Crumble bars
1 licorice strap
24 dark Choc Bits

1 Preheat oven to 180°C/160°C fan-forced; line 12-hole (⅓-cup/80ml) muffin pan with paper cases.

2 Make cake according to directions on packet; divide mixture evenly among paper cases. Bake about 20 minutes. Stand cakes 5 minutes before turning, top-side up, onto wire rack to cool.

3 Meanwhile, make butter cream. Spread cakes with butter cream.

4 Cut Violet Crumble bars into thin shards. Cut licorice into 12 small triangles for noses; cut remaining licorice into strips to make whiskers and mouths. Using picture as a guide, position licorice on cakes to make face; use Choc Bits for eyes. Position crumble bar shards around cakes to make lions' manes.

butter cream Beat butter in small bowl with an electric mixer until as white as possible. Gradually beat in half the sifted icing sugar then milk and remaining sifted icing sugar. Tint butter cream with caramel colouring.

preparation time 40 minutes
cooking time 20 minutes
makes 12
notes Cakes can be made one day ahead; store in an airtight container. Cakes can be completed up to three hours ahead; keep refrigerated if the weather is hot. Cooked cakes can be frozen for up to one month. Thaw cakes at room temperature for about three hours.

butterfly fairy bread

60g butter, softened
12 large slices white sandwich bread (540g)
6cm butterfly cutter
6 musk sticks, halved lengthways
½ cup hundreds and thousands

1 Spread butter on one side of each bread slice. Using butterfly cutter, cut out three butterflies from each slice.
2 Cut each musk stick into 2cm lengths; place one piece of musk stick in centre of each butterfly.
3 Sprinkle hundreds and thousands into small shallow dish; gently press each butterfly, buttered-side down, into hundreds and thousands. Place on serving plate.

preparation time 15 minutes
makes 36
note Recipe can be made up to three hours ahead; keep covered.

microphone ice-creams

45cm licorice strap
12 square-based ice-cream cones
2 litres vanilla ice-cream
edible silver glitter
chocolate topping
400g dark eating chocolate, chopped coarsely
⅓ cup (80ml) vegetable oil

1 Cut licorice strap into three 15cm lengths; cut each length into 4 strips.
2 Using skewer, make a small hole near the base of each cone (not through the bottom, otherwise the cones won't stand up). Push end of licorice strip into each hole for microphone lead.
3 Push some ice-cream firmly into cones to hold licorice in place. Fill cones with ice-cream until level with tops of cones.
4 Using ice-cream scoop, top cones with ice-cream domes. Place cones on tray; freeze about 10 minutes or until firm.
5 Meanwhile, make chocolate topping.
6 Pour topping into small deep bowl; dip ice-cream domes into chocolate, sprinkle with glitter. Return cones to freezer until required.
chocolate topping Melt ingredients in small saucepan over low heat until smooth.

preparation time 20 minutes (+ freezing time)
makes 12
notes Cones can be made up to three days ahead.
Edible glitter is available from specialist cake decorating shops.

jam starlets

2 sheets ready-rolled shortcrust pastry
⅔ cup (220g) strawberry jam

1 Preheat oven to 180°C/160°C fan-forced. Grease two 12-hole
(1½ tablespoons/30ml) shallow round-based patty pans.
2 Cut out 24 x 6cm stars and 24 x 1cm stars from pastry.
3 Place large stars into pans; drop level teaspoons of jam into pastry
cases. Place small stars on patty pan in spaces between the holes.
4 Bake about 15 minutes. Remove tarts from pans onto wire rack while
still hot; place small pastry stars on top of jam. Cool.

preparation time 10 minutes
cooking time 15 minutes
makes 24
note Tarts can be made one day ahead; store, in a single layer, in an
airtight container.

candied popcorn

2 tablespoons vegetable oil
½ cup (110g) popping corn
2 cups (440g) caster sugar
1 cup (250ml) water
½ teaspoon pink food colouring

1 Heat oil in large heavy-based saucepan; cook corn over high heat, covered with a tight-fitting lid, shaking pan occasionally, until popping stops. Transfer to large bowl.
2 Combine sugar, the water and colouring in medium heavy-based frying pan; stir over heat, without boiling, until sugar is dissolved. Bring to the boil; boil, uncovered, without stirring, about 15 minutes or until a teaspoon of mixture cracks when dropped into a glass of cold water.
3 Remove pan from heat; when bubbles subside, add popcorn. Stir popcorn to coat with toffee mixture.
4 When popcorn mixture has candied, spread onto a foil-lined oven tray to cool.

preparation time 5 minutes (+ cooling time)
cooking time 25 minutes
makes 6 cups
note Popcorn can be made two days ahead; store in an airtight container.

cornflake cakes

75g butter
⅓ cup (115g) honey
1 tablespoon caster sugar
5 cups (200g) corn flakes

1 Preheat oven to 180°C/160°C fan-forced. Line two 12-hole (⅓-cup/80ml) muffin pans with paper cases.
2 Combine butter, honey and sugar in small saucepan; stir over heat until mixture is smooth.
3 Place corn flakes in large bowl, add butter mixture; stir until corn flakes are well coated.
4 Divide corn flake mixture among paper cases; bake, in oven, 8 minutes. Stand 15 minutes or until firm.

preparation time 10 minutes (+ standing time)
cooking time 10 minutes
makes 24
note Recipe can be made one day ahead; store in an airtight container.

disco cake

3 x 340g packets buttercake
  mix
30cm x 46cm prepared board,
  covered with decorative
  greaseproof paper
butter cream (see method)
pink food colouring
decorations
red, yellow, orange and green
  fruit rings
red, yellow, orange, green and
  purple "fruit salad" soft jellies
red, yellow, orange, green
  and purple jelly beans
red, yellow, orange, green
  and purple mixed lollies
red, yellow, orange, green
  and purple Smarties
2cm silver disco ball
silver edible glitter
4 x 30cm silver pipe cleaners
  (tinsel sticks)

1 Preheat oven to 180°C/160°C fan-forced;
grease and line deep 26cm x 36cm baking dish.
2 Make cakes according to packet directions,
pour into dish; bake about 1 hour. Stand cake
20 minutes then turn, top-side up, onto wire
rack to cool.
3 Using serrated knife, level cake top. Place
cake, cut-side down, on prepared board.
4 Make butter cream; spread all over cake.
5 Mark out the letters "DISCO" with a skewer.
Sort lollies into five small bowls according
to colour.
6 Using one colour for each letter, arrange
lollies, overlapping, pressing to secure to cake.
Position disco ball above the "i". Sprinkle
edible glitter all over top of cake.
7 Position pipe cleaners around base of cake.
butter cream Beat 250g softened butter
with electric mixer until as white as possible.
Gradually beat in 1½ cups sifted icing sugar and
⅓ cup milk then an extra 1½ cups icing sugar.
Use food colouring to tint butter cream pink.

preparation time 45 minutes
cooking time 1 hour
serves 24
notes Cooked cake can be frozen for up
to one month. Thaw at room temperature for
about six hours. Edible glitter is available from
specialist cake decorating shops. Long (30cm)
pipe cleaners (tinsel sticks), are available from
craft stores, as is the small disco ball.

jellyfish

2 x 340g packets buttercake
mix
4 x 85g packets
blue jelly crystals
butter cream (see method)
green food colouring
decorations
1 white marshmallow,
halved widthways
1 egg shell, halved,
washed, dried
2 blue Smarties
9 rainbow straps
fish lollies
raspberries lollies
plastic coral

notes You need a 35cm x
45cm plastic tray for this
recipe. Cooked cake can be
frozen for up to one month;
thaw at room temperature
for about six hours. Jelly and
cake can be completed a day
ahead. Refrigerate separately.
Position cake, tentacles and
decorations in tray up to three
hours ahead. Refrigerate cake
until required.

preparation time 1¼ hours
cooking time 1 hour
serves 18

1   Preheat oven to 180°C/160°C fan-forced;
grease and line deep 26cm x 33cm baking dish.
2   Make cakes according to packet directions,
pour into dish; bake about 1 hour. Stand cake
20 minutes then turn, top-side up, onto wire
rack to cool.
3   Dissolve jellies in large heatproof bowl using
3 cups (750ml) boiling water and 2½ cups
(625ml) cold water. Refrigerate until set.
4   Using serrated knife, level top of cake; turn
cut-side down. Using picture as a guide, cut
jellyfish shape from cake. Place in 35cm x 45cm
plastic tray (if it's metal, line with foil).
5   Make butter cream; spread all over cake.
6   Cut two hollows for jellyfish's eye sockets.
Place marshmallow halves into each egg shell;
secure Smarties to marshmallows with a little
butter cream. Using picture as a guide, position
eyes on cake. Cut a blue strip from one rainbow
strap; position on cake for jellyfish's mouth.
7   Using whisk, break up jelly; spoon carefully
into tray around cake.
8   Using picture as a guide, position remaining
rainbow straps as tentacles. Decorate jelly with
raspberries, fish and coral.
butter cream Beat 250g soft butter with
electric mixer until as white as possible.
Gradually beat in 1½ cups sifted icing sugar
and ⅓ cup milk then an extra 1½ cups sifted
icing sugar. Use food colouring to tint butter
cream green.

shooting star

5 x 340g packets buttercake
 mix
38cm-square prepared board,
 covered with decorative
 greaseproof paper
white chocolate frosting
300ml thickened cream
2 cups (360g) white eating
 chocolate, chopped
 coarsely
toffee shards
3 cups (660g) caster sugar
1½ cups (375ml) water

notes Cut a star from gold
cardboard and place on the
centre of the cake.
Freeze un-iced cooked cake
for up to one month. Thaw at
room temperature for six hours.
The toffee mixture is drizzled
between two lines drawn
12cm apart. Shards will hold
their shape for up to eight hours,
depending on the humidity.

preparation time 2 hours
(+ standing, cooling and
refrigeration time)
cooking time 2¾ hours
serves 30

1 Preheat oven to 160°C/140°C fan-forced.
Grease deep 30cm-square cake pan; line
base and sides with baking paper.
2 Make cakes according to packet directions;
pour into pan. Bake about 2½ hours. Stand
cake 20 minutes then turn, top-side up, onto
wire rack to cool.
3 Make white chocolate frosting.
4 Make toffee shards.
5 Level cake top with serrated knife then turn
cut-side down. Using picture as a guide, cut
a large star shape from cake; place on board
cut-side down. Spread frosting all over cake.
6 Cut a gold star just smaller than top of cake
and position on cake. Position toffee shards
around sides of star.

white chocolate frosting Boil cream in small
saucepan, remove from heat; add chocolate,
stir until smooth. Refrigerate about 2 hours or
until mixture is spreadable, stirring occasionally.

toffee shards Line four oven trays with baking
paper; mark two lines on each sheet of paper,
12cm apart; turn paper so markings are
underneath. Combine sugar and the water in
small saucepan; stir over heat, without boiling,
until sugar dissolves. Bring to the boil then
reduce heat; simmer, uncovered, without
stirring, about 15 minutes or until toffee is
golden brown. Remove from heat; allow
bubbles to subside. Using wooden spoon,
drizzle toffee between lines on baking paper.
Stand at room temperature until set. Shards
can be positioned around cake up to eight
hours before serving.

sweetheart cake

2 x 340g packets buttercake
    mix
butter cream (see method)
pink and red food colouring
48cm x 55cm board, covered
    with decorative
        greaseproof paper
decorations
pink and white mallow bakes,
    halved
raspberry lollies
small red jubes, cut in half
red fruit rings
pink and red jelly beans
pink and white marshmallows
musk sticks

notes Cooked cupcakes can
be frozen for up to one month.
Thaw at room temperature
for about three hours, then
ice and decorate the cakes
with sweets.

We used 25 cakes to make
the heart, but you can use as
many cakes as you like. Use
the remainder for the party or
freeze for later.

1 Preheat oven to 180°C/160°C fan-forced.
Line four 12-hole (⅓-cup/80ml) muffin pans
with red paper patty cases.

2 Make cakes according to packet directions;
divide mixture evenly among cases. Bake about
20 minutes. Stand cakes 5 minutes before
turning, top-side up, onto wire racks to cool.

3 Meanwhile, make butter cream.

4 Tint one-third of the butter cream pink,
tint another third red; leave remaining butter
cream plain.

5 Spread one-third of the cakes with pink
butter cream, one-third with red butter cream
and remaining cakes with plain butter cream.

6 Using picture as a guide, decorate cakes
with lollies, as desired.

7 Arrange cupcakes, side by side, on board,
in the shape of a heart. Use musk sticks to
outline the heart shape.

butter cream Beat 250g softened butter in a
small bowl with an electric mixer until as white
as possible. Gradually beat in 1½ cups sifted
icing sugar and ⅓ cup milk, then an extra
1½ cups sifted icing sugar.

preparation time 50 minutes
(+ standing and cooling time)
cooking time 20 minutes
serves 48

spooky raspberry ice-cream cake

3 x 340g packets buttercake
  mix
36cm x 46cm prepared board,
  covered with decorative
  greaseproof paper
2 litres vanilla ice-cream
300g frozen raspberries
6 egg whites
1⅓ cups (295g) caster sugar
⅓ cup (80ml) strawberry
  topping
2 tablespoons chocolate
  topping
2 strawberry and cream lollies

notes We used two small
shallow round ovenproof
bowls about 4cm in diameter
and one small shallow oval
ovenproof bowl about 9cm
long to make the ghost's
eyes and mouth.
Make the meringue 30 minutes
before serving the cake.
Cake and ice-cream can be
prepared, ready for meringue,
up to one week ahead. Keep,
covered in foil, in the freezer.

preparation time 1½ hours
(+ standing and freezing time)
cooking time 1 hour
serves 24

1 Preheat oven to 180°C/160°C fan-forced.
Grease and line deep 26cm x 36cm baking dish.
2 Make cakes according to packet directions,
pour into dish; bake about 1 hour. Stand
20 minutes then turn, top-side up, onto wire
rack to cool.
3 Level cake top with serrated knife. Turn cake
cut-side down. Using picture as a guide, cut
ghost shape from cake. Place, cut-side down,
on board; discard remaining cake. Freeze cake
for 3 hours.
4 Soften ice-cream slightly in large bowl; stir
in raspberries. Return ice-cream to container;
return to freezer until ice-cream is frozen.
5 Remove cake from freezer; position small
round and oval bowls for eyes and mouth (see
note, left).
6 Scoop out ice-cream using large ice-cream
scoop; place scoops all over top of frozen cake
and close to the bowls to hold them in place.
Freeze cake about 1 hour or until ice-cream
is frozen.
7 Preheat oven to 220°C/200°C fan-forced.
8 Beat egg whites with electric mixer until soft
peaks form; gradually add sugar, 1 tablespoon
at a time, beating until sugar is dissolved
between additions.
9 Spread meringue all over cake, leaving
bowls uncovered. Bake about 2 minutes or
until meringue feels firm.
10 Fill eye cavities with strawberry topping and
mouth cavity with chocolate topping. Place
one strawberry and cream lolly in each eye
socket; serve immediately.

handbag

3 x 340g packets buttercake
    mix
38cm-square prepared board,
    covered with decorative
    greaseproof paper
butter cream (see method)
pink food colouring
decorations
28cm black licorice strap
2 square red jubes, cut in half
silver and pink cachous
5 large pink and black licorice
    allsorts, halved

preparation time 1 hour
(+ standing time)
cooking time 1 hour
serves 18

1 Preheat oven to 180°C/160°C fan-forced.
Grease deep 24cm x 35cm baking dish; line
with baking paper.

2 Make cakes according to packet directions,
pour into dish; bake about 1 hour. Stand cake
20 minutes then turn, top-side up, onto wire
rack to cool.

3 Level cake top with serrated knife then turn
cut-side down. Using picture as a guide, cut
handbag and handle pieces from cake. Place
handbag on board, cut-side down, leaving
space for handle. Using skewer, and picture
as a guide, mark inner section of the handbag
onto cake.

4 Make butter cream.

5 Tint a quarter of the butter cream dark pink;
tint remaining pale pink. Using picture as a
guide, spread butter cream over handbag.

6 Spread handle pieces with the pale pink
butter cream; position handle on cake and
smooth joins.

7 Cut licorice strap into thin strips; position
on cake, as pictured.

8 Position silver cachous and jubes, cut-sides
up, on cake for clasp.

9 Mark out the name of the birthday girl with
pink cachous.

10 Decorate handle with allsorts.

butter cream Beat 250g softened butter
with electric mixer until as white as possible.
Gradually beat in 1½ cups sifted icing sugar
and ⅓ cup milk then an extra 1½ cups sifted
icing sugar.

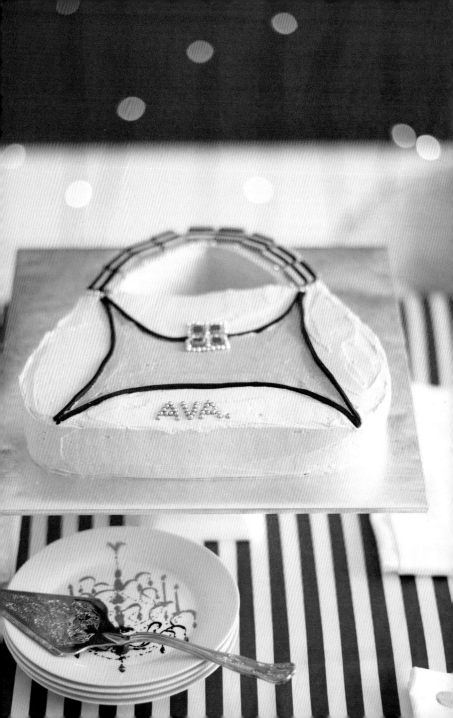

glossary

bacon rashers also known as bacon slices.

bean sprouts also known as bean shoots; tender new growths of assorted beans and seeds germinated for consumption as sprouts.

beetroot also known as red beets; round root vegetable.

bicarbonate of soda also known as baking or carb soda.

biscuits, plain sweet also known as cookies.

bread
  bake at home dinner rolls partially-baked bread only needing a few minutes in the oven to give fresh-baked rolls.
  lavash flat, unleavened bread of Mediterranean origin.
  tortilla thin, unleavened, round bread originating in Mexico. Two kinds are available, one made from wheat flour and the other from corn.

breadcrumbs stale one- or two-day-old bread made into crumbs by grating, blending or processing.

butter use salted or unsalted (sweet) butter; 125g is equal to one stick (4oz) of butter.

cachous also called dragées in some countries; minuscule (3mm to 5mm) metallic-looking, but edible, confectionery balls used in cake decorating; available in silver, gold or various colours.

capsicum also known as bell pepper or, simply, pepper. Discard membranes and seeds before use.

cheese
  baby bocconcini from the diminutive of "boccone", meaning mouthful in Italian; walnut-sized, baby mozzarella. A delicate, semi-soft, white cheese traditionally made from buffalo milk.
  pizza a commercial blend of grated mozzarella, cheddar and parmesan.

cream cheese commonly known as Philadelphia or Philly, a soft cows-milk cheese. Also available as spreadable light cream cheese, a blend of cottage and cream cheeses.

chilli, red thai small, medium hot, and bright red in colour.

chocolate
  dark eating made with cocoa liquor, cocoa butter and sugar.
  Melts discs of compounded chocolate ideal for melting and moulding.
  white eating contains no cocoa solids but derives its sweet flavour from cocoa butter. Very sensitive to heat.

cream
  sour a thick commercially-cultured soured cream.
  thickened a whipping cream containing a thickener. Minimum fat content 35%.

cucumber, lebanese short, slender and thin-skinned. Probably the most popular variety because of its tender, edible skin, tiny, yielding seeds, and sweet, fresh flavoursome taste.

dijon mustard a pale brown, distinctively flavoured, fairly mild french mustard.

flour, plain an all-purpose flour made from wheat.

ginger also known as green or root ginger; the thick root of a tropical plant.
  ground also known as powdered ginger; used as a flavouring in cakes, pies and puddings but cannot be substituted for fresh ginger.

golden syrup a by-product of refined sugar cane; pure maple syrup or honey can be substituted.

hundreds and thousands nonpareils; tiny sugar-syrup-coated sugar crystals that come in a variety of colours and are used to decorate cakes and party foods.

jam also known as preserve or conserve; most often made from fruit.

jelly crystals a powdered mixture of artificial fruit, gelatine, sweetener and flavouring used to make a moulded, translucent, quivering dessert. Also known as jello.

lettuce, iceberg a crisp, heavy, firm, round lettuce with tightly packed leaves.

lollies a confectionery also known as sweets or candy.

mallow bakes very small marshmallows.

mesclun mixed baby salad leaves; also sold as salad mix or gourmet salad mix.

mince also ground meat.

onions

  green also known as scallion or, incorrectly, shallot; an immature onion picked before the bulb has formed, having a long, bright-green edible stalk.

  red also known as spanish, red spanish or bermuda onion; a sweet-flavoured, large, purple-red onion.

pancetta cured pork belly; bacon can be substituted.

parsley, flat-leaf also known as continental parsley or italian parsley.

pastry, ready-rolled sheets of puff or shortcrust pastry, available from supermarkets.

pesto, sun-dried tomato a thick paste made from sun-dried tomatoes, oil, vinegar and herbs.

refried beans pinto or borlotti beans that are cooked twice; first soaked and boiled, then mashed and fried. Available canned in supermarkets.

rice paper sheets also known as banh trang. Made from rice paste and stamped into rounds; stores well at room temperature. Are used as wrappers for food; make good spring-roll wrappers.

rice vermicelli also known as sen mee, mei fun or bee hoon. These noodles are used throughout Asia in spring rolls and cold salads; similar to bean threads.

sauces

  barbecue a spicy, tomato-based sauce used to marinate or as a condiment.

  fish also called nam pla or nuoc nam; made from pulverised salted fermented fish, most often anchovies. Has a pungent smell and strong taste; use sparingly.

  oyster this rich, brown sauce is made from oysters and their brine, cooked with salt and soy sauce, and thickened with starches.

  sweet chilli a comparatively mild, Thai-type sauce made from red chillies, sugar, garlic and vinegar.

  tomato also known as ketchup or catsup; made from tomatoes, vinegar and spices.

  worcestershire thin, dark-brown, spicy sauce used as a seasoning for meat.

spring roll wrappers also called egg roll wrappers; can be purchased fresh or frozen. A wheat-based pastry used for making gow gee and samosas, as well as spring rolls.

sugar we used coarse, granulated table sugar, also known as crystal sugar, unless otherwise specified.

  brown an extremely soft, finely granulated sugar retaining molasses for its characteristic colour and flavour.

  caster also known as superfine or finely granulated table sugar.

  icing sugar also known as confectioners' sugar or powdered sugar; granulated sugar crushed together with a small amount of added cornflour.

  pure icing sugar also known as confectioners' sugar or powdered sugar, but has no added cornflour.

sultanas dried grapes, also known as golden raisins.

sweetened condensed milk milk from which 60% of the water had been removed; the remaining milk is then sweetened with sugar.

vanilla extract beans that have been submerged in alcohol. Vanilla essence is not a suitable substitute.

vinegar white made from spirit of cane sugar.

wombok also known as chinese cabbage, peking or napa cabbage; elongated in shape with pale green, crinkly leaves, this is the most common cabbage in South-East Asia.

zucchini also known as courgette; small, pale- or dark-green, yellow or white vegetable belonging to the squash family.

conversion chart

MEASURES

One Australian metric measuring cup holds approximately 250ml, one Australian metric tablespoon holds 20ml, one Australian metric teaspoon holds 5ml.

The difference between one country's measuring cups and another's is within a 2- or 3-teaspoon variance, and will not affect your cooking results. North America, New Zealand and the United Kingdom use a 15ml tablespoon. All cup and spoon measurements are level. The most accurate way of measuring dry ingredients is to weigh them. When measuring liquids, use a clear glass or plastic jug with metric markings.

We use large eggs with an average weight of 60g.

DRY MEASURES

METRIC	IMPERIAL
15g	½oz
30g	1oz
60g	2oz
90g	3oz
125g	4oz (¼lb)
155g	5oz
185g	6oz
220g	7oz
250g	8oz (½lb)
280g	9oz
315g	10oz
345g	11oz
375g	12oz (¾lb)
410g	13oz
440g	14oz
470g	15oz
500g	16oz (1lb)
750g	24oz (1½lb)
1kg	32oz (2lb)

LIQUID MEASURES

METRIC	IMPERIAL
30ml	1 fluid oz
60ml	2 fluid oz
100ml	3 fluid oz
125ml	4 fluid oz
150ml	5 fluid oz (¼ pint/1 gill)
190ml	6 fluid oz
250ml	8 fluid oz
300ml	10 fluid oz (½ pint)
500ml	16 fluid oz
600ml	20 fluid oz (1 pint)
1000ml (1 litre)	1¾ pints

LENGTH MEASURES

METRIC	IMPERIAL
3mm	⅛in
6mm	¼in
1cm	½in
2cm	¾in
2.5cm	1in
5cm	2in
6cm	2½in
8cm	3in
10cm	4in
13cm	5in
15cm	6in
18cm	7in
20cm	8in
23cm	9in
25cm	10in
28cm	11in
30cm	12in (1ft)

OVEN TEMPERATURES

These oven temperatures are only a guide for conventional ovens. For fan-forced ovens, check the manufacturer's manual.

	°C (CELSIUS)	°F (FAHRENHEIT)	GAS MARK
Very slow	120	250	½
Slow	150	275-300	1-2
Moderately slow	160	325	3
Moderate	180	350-375	4-5
Moderately hot	200	400	6
Hot	220	425-450	7-8
Very hot	240	475	9

index

TEST KITCHEN
Food director Pamela Clark
Recipe editor Louise Patniotis

ACP BOOKS
General manager Christine Whiston
Editorial director Susan Tomnay
Creative director Hieu Chi Nguyen
Designer Melissa Deare
Senior editor Wendy Bryant
Director of sales Brian Cearnes
Marketing manager Bridget Cody
Business analyst Rebecca Varela
Operations manager David Scotto
Production manager Victoria Jefferys
International rights enquiries Laura Bamford
lbamford@acpuk.com

ACP Books are published by ACP Magazines
a division of PBL Media Pty Limited
Publishing director, Women's lifestyle Pat Ingram
Director of sales, Women's lifestyle Lynette Phillips
Commercial manager, Women's lifestyle Seymour Cohen
Marketing director, Women's lifestyle Matthew Dominello
Public relations manager, Women's lifestyle Hannah Deveraux
Creative director, Events, Women's lifestyle Luke Bonnano
Research Director, Women's lifestyle Justin Stone
PBL Media, Chief Executive Officer Ian Law

Cover Hedgehog slice, page 34
Photographer John Paul Urizar
Stylist Sarah DeNardi
Food preparation Angela Muscat

Back cover at left, Mini pizzas with 3 toppings, page 6;
at right, Strawberry & cream meringues, page 30.

Produced by ACP Books, Sydney.
Published by ACP Books,
a division of ACP Magazines Ltd,
54 Park St, Sydney; GPO Box 4088,
Sydney, NSW 2001
phone (02) 9282 8618 fax (02) 9267 9438.
acpbooks@acpmagazines.com.au
www.acpbooks.com.au
Printed by Dai Nippon in Korea.
Australia Distributed by Network Services,
phone +61 2 9282 8777 fax +61 2 9264 3278
networkweb@networkservicescompany.com.au
United Kingdom Distributed by Australian Consolidated Press (UK),
phone (01604) 642 200 fax (01604) 642 300 books@acpuk.com
New Zealand Distributed by Netlink Distribution Company,
phone (9) 366 9966 ask@ndc.co.nz
South Africa Distributed by PSD Promotions,
phone (27 11) 392 6065/6/7 fax (27 11) 392 6079/80 orders@psdprom.co.za
Canada Distributed by Publishers Group Canada
phone (800) 663 5714 fax (800) 565 3770 service@raincoast.com

A catalogue record for this book is available
from the British Library.
ISBN: 978 1 86396 883 6 (pbk.)
© ACP Magazines Ltd 2008
ABN 18 053 273 546

Send recipe enquiries to:
recipeenquiries@acpmagazines.com.au